Solving for X

Poems

Maryfrances Wagner

Missouri Poet Laureate 2021 - 2023

Solving for X reveals a poet, image by dazzling image, trying to solve the old equation of what makes a life worth living. Textured and quirky in the best way, these poems of lovers, family, and the natural world are full of the beauty of a life well-lived, with all the questions still open.

    Catherine Anderson, author of *The Work of Hands*

"I'm from red sauce, garlic, and fig trees," writes Maryfrances Wagner. An Italian world re-created in Kansas City is her childhood, and this informs her rich poetry filled with wry humor and wisdom. She tells stories, describes recipes, weddings, wine club, and family card games. The poet amplifies attractive and accessible moments with original, surprising language. She blends story and song masterfully. *Solving for X* might be my favorite book from this talented writer—so far!

    Denise Low, 2007-09 Kansas Poet Laureate, winner Red Mountain Press Editor's Choice Award

Edited by Jason Ryberg

Copyright © 2022 by Maryfrances Wagner

LCCN: 2022934591

ISBN: 978-1-952411-97-7

Published by Spartan Press

First Edition

Layout and Design by Greg Field

Cover Design by Maryfrances Wagner and Greg Field

Photos by Greg Field

Collages by Maryfrances Wagner

Acknowledgments

Special thanks to the editors who chose these poems for publication.

As It Ought To Be: "Dreaming through Covid," "Losing Cousin Carolyn," "Love Should Be More Like Yarrow," *Coal City Review*: "Fabulous Realities," *Curating Home* (Woodneath Poetry Center): "I Am," "Ode to a Male Seahorse," *Dying Dahlia*: "Saturdays at the Bakery," *Evening Street Review*: "Mushroom Squad," "The Deer," *Flint Hills Review*: "Cheap Concert Seats," *Glass*: "Myotis Lucifugus," *I-70 Review*: (poem as collage): "Island," "August in Kansas City," "Corvus Albus," "Take the Sea," "Stay Close," *Journal of American Poetry*: "Fracture," "Raccoon on the Path," *Main Street Rag*: "At the Allen Ginsberg Poetry Reading," "Disappearing," *Naugatuck River Review*: "Girls at the Sea Aquarium," *Paddock Review*: "Because I Never Learned Calculus," *Patterson Literary Review*: "Last Six Months," *Red River Review*: "Rain Elegy," *River Styx*: "Stuttering Hands," *Rusty Truck*: "Barbed," "Auld Lange Syne's End of Set," *Salt*: "Wine Access Club," "Lelia's Hair Museum," *South Florida Poetry Review*: "Children Should Be Seen and Not Heard," "Women Talk of Men They've Known," *San Pedro River Review*: "The Out-of-Town Family Wedding," *Tar River Review*: "My Neighbor, Mary Grace, at Six, Paints Jack-o'-lanterns in Her Driveway," *Thorny Locust*: "The Drexlers," "Fortune Tellers," "Naked," "Jackson Pollock's One," "Pogo Cat Haibun," "Close to the Bone," "Thinning the Herd," "Will," "Unwritten Rules," "Wedding Bouquets," *Voices In Italian Americana*: "Cataract Surgery," *Vox Populi*: "Chuck," "Prompt," and "After Adopting Sylvie," *Green Mountains Literary Review*: "Pomegranate," "Rabbits," "Lost in Snow," "Cropping," "House Dreaming," and "Those Left Behind," *Concho River Review*: "Ends," *The Mantle Poetry*, "For What We Don't Know."

"Missouri" is the 2021 Missouri Poet Laureate State Poem, read at

Acknowledgments

the Missouri Capitol for the Bicentennial Celebration and published on the Missouri Arts Council website.

Also a special thanks to the editors who nominated several of these poems for a Pushcart Prize.

Thanks to all of those who have supported and helped me in some way on this journey: Robert Stewart, Lola Haskins, Jo McDougall, Alice Friman, Catherine Anderson, Denise Low, Tina Hacker, Alarie Tennille, Ann Slegman, Jemshed Khan, Jason Ryberg, Christopher Buckley, Brian Daldorph, Jenny Molberg, Susan Whitmore, Teresa Godsey, Annie Newcomer, Gary Lechliter, Jason Browne, William Trowbridge, M. Scott Douglass, Scot Young, Michael Simms, Luke Whisnant, Silvia Kofler, Phyllis Becker, Pat Lawson, Judith Roberts, Janice Yocum, Frank Higgins, Linda Fishell, Janette Williams, Bonnie Anderson, Keith Anderson, Marianne Kunkel, Hyejung Kook, Ruth Williams, Al Ortolani, Hadara Bar-Nadav, Ronda Miller, Andrés Rodríguez, Andrea Brookhart, Maria Vasquez Boyd, Angela Elam, Barbara Loots, Jan Rog, Lindsey Martin-Bowen, Sue Trowbridge, Lisa Stewart, Joe Benevento, Patricia Cleary Miller, Richard Robert Hanson, Gay Dust, and especially my husband Greg Field, the love and support of my life. A special thanks also to all of those friends and fellow writers that are too numerous to name but have been a part of my writing life in some way. You know who you are. So many walk through our lives and sometimes don't realize their impact whether it's directly or indirectly.

Table of Contents

I

I Am	1
Stuttering Hands	2
Children Should Be Seen and Not Heard	3
Ace of Spades	4
Rain Elegy	5
Close to the Bone	6
Because I Never Learned Calculus	7
Chuck	8
Mark	10
Ode to a Male Seahorse	11
Girls at the Sea Aquarium	12
At the Allen Ginsberg Poetry Reading	13
Cheap Concert Seats	14
Thinning the Herd	15
Mother Suite:	17
Last Six Months	17
After the Transfusion	18
Chemo	19
Afterward	20
Nulliparous	21
The Out of Town Family Wedding	22
Wedding Bouquets	23
The Drexlers	24
My Neighbor, Mary Grace, at Six Years Old, Paints Jack-o'lanterns	25
Pomegranate	26
Cropping	27
Prompt	28
Brandon Langford Talks through Detention	30
Disappearing	31
Ends	33
Lelia's Hair Museum	34
Love Should Be More Like Yarrow	35

Saturdays at the Bakery	36
Women Talk of Men They've Known	37
Cataract Surgery	38
Fracture	39
Unwritten Rules	40
Barbed	42
Losing Cousin Carolyn	43
Dreaming through Covid	44
House Dreaming	45
Socially Distancing We Buy Plants Too Early	47
Auld Lange Syne's End of Set	48
Fortune Tellers	49
Wine Access Club	50
Lost in the Snow	52

II

Jackson Pollock's 1	54
Island	56
August	58

III

Missouri	62
Garage Pantry Moths	65
Rain Haibun	66
The Pogo Cat Haibun	67
Will	68
For What We Don't Know	69
Naked	70
Fabulous Realities	71
Ghost Forest	73
After Adopting Sylvie	74
Rabbits	75
The Deer	76
Mushroom Squad	77
Those Left Behind	78
Myotis Lucifugus	79
Raccoon on the Path	81

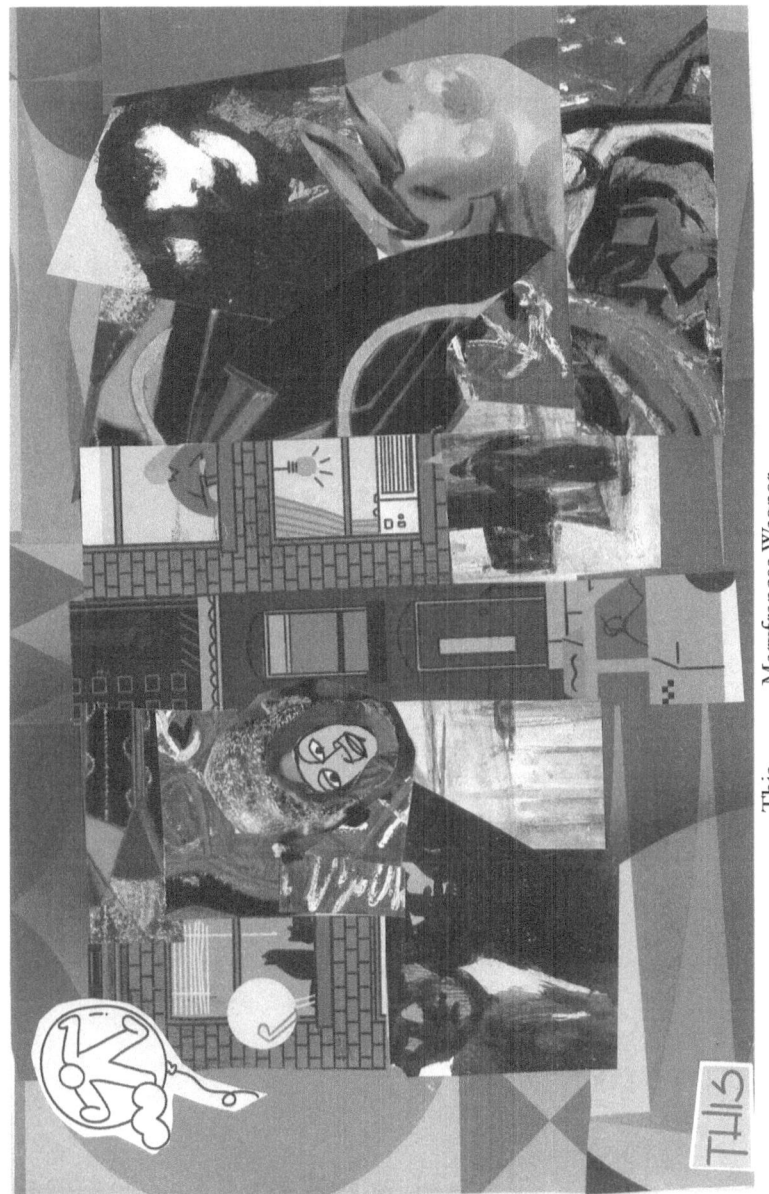

This   Maryfrances Wagner

I

I'm from red sauce, garlic, and fig trees

I Am

I'm from red sauce, garlic, and fig trees,
mantiglie, wine barrels, and Frank's Jewelry.
My zie told stories, grew basil, made cannoli.
My Nonno loved *O Solo Mio*, Da Vinci, La Cappella Sistina.
I'm from calamari, carciofi, Scimeca's salsiccia,
Sunday pasta, Christmas sphingi, homemade anisette,
from Maria and Antonio, Bessie and Frank, Salvatore
and Marguerite. I'm from si mangia, vieni qui,
and ciao, Nonna's calloused knees and rosaries.
I'm from Kansas City, Palermo, Bivona, and Florence,
the sea and the mountains, goats and herbs, Zio Nene's
grin, Nonna's gardenias, Nanno's mandolin. I'm from
floors you can eat on, stiff towels dried on lines, sinks
scrubbed to a perfect shine. I'm from homemade
ricotta, glistening olive oil, late-night wakes, tatted lace,
bread boards passed down, the ship *Germania*, from roots
without soil, the one left standing, waiting for a place.

Stuttering Hands

Unlike Salvador Dali, I don't remember
the womb. Unlike Gunter Grass, I don't

remember the birth canal. I remember
porches. Squeaky gliders. Busy gutters.

Frosty sherbet in the darkness of distant
stars, stingy breezes, and misled rain.

The houses where we lived are now
empty lots waiting for urban renewal.

Our breath moved through hallways
of lost ghosts while we slept. I remember

Cusumano mispronounced over and over,
hot shame ringing like bells. I remember

a dozen red pencils my mother gave me,
engraved with my name. All but one

disappeared. The next school year,
a teacher wrote me a pass with one

of the pencils, my name in her hand,
the teacher who asked me in class

if I ate pasta every day and could my
family talk without using their hands.

Children Should Be Seen and Not Heard

We learned to fold our hands in our laps
like small cabbages, sit up straight, and look

intent. Adults thought we listened well,
but we blinked and imagined ourselves

aloft on a Ferris wheel. Sometimes our heads
took us home to the toy chest with a box

of Lucky Charms or into the neighbor's yard
picking the ripest cherries. Of course, we

returned for slices of pound cake or ice cream
with chocolate sauce. If they told us to play

outside, we never screamed and knew how
to stay clean even if we played tag or smeared

lightning bugs on our arms. We heard about
Aunt Sylvia stuck in an elevator, Uncle Ray's

bout with a bottle of gin, Aunt Josie's black eye.
We kept silent and recited "Jabberwocky"

in our heads or calculated how many times
we'd have to rake leaves or fold laundry

to buy a hermit crab. When our fathers
gathered their gloves and our mothers their purses,

we stacked our puzzles, zipped our backpacks,
and gave everyone a stiff hug, our eyes crossed

and holding our breath while smashed into them,
then carried ourselves quietly out the door.

Ace of Spades

The grownups played pinochle
for pennies. We kids played
monopoly in my cousin's room
with its dim lamp on a broken
end table. If all went well, we
hugged goodbye at ten. The night
a potato chip broke between
my aunt's teeth and sprayed the air,
interrupting her husband's next play, he
jerked up and backhanded her. Blood
gushed below her eye. Her lipsticked
glass was a thousand scattered frowns.
My father overturned the table
and slugged him. My uncle stumbled
into the bedroom from where I watched
and found my cousin mumbling to her
Barbie. He slapped her. She squeezed
her eyes shut and didn't move except for
the swish of her ponytail. Her brother
rolled a six, landed on Park Place, but his
sister was dark silence, mute as a table leg.
Her father hit her again and left. She
whispered to Barbie, and we sat
frozen until my father, his shadow
beating him through the doorway,
reached out his hand.

Rain Elegy

All night the dog whined through strikes
and flashes while rain pelted the skylight
and sang through our gutters.

Morning hung over with lost limbs,
petals stuck to the patio, I steered
the dog across soggy yard, past runoff.

I remembered the summer the flood
sucked your car into the lake. One hand
dangled from the window when they

hauled you out. The dog stared at standing
water and strained on her leash to go back.
A beheaded tuberose spread far its thick scent.

Close to the Bone

Once a mansion with a winding staircase,
brocaded drapes, and a chandeliered parlor.

Later, a boarding house—one-room
apartments, hot plates behind curtains.

A room with a bed, two chairs, small
wardrobe and dresser for life's collections—

a Bible, newspaper clippings, necklaces on hooks,
earrings or cuff links in a chipped candy dish.

Louver doors divided each room
with open space at the bottom—

not a chance any word spoken
would go unheard. Easy to see feet shuffle.

Warm evenings, boarders sat
on the front porch to enjoy cool air,

to talk about working in a warehouse,
sewing uniforms, typing. On cold nights,

they gathered around one television. Some
had a radio they played in the afternoon.

They shared a bathroom on each floor. Jodie lived
in the top floor attic room with her father and six brothers,

two dresses, no winter coat, one pair of black flats
and a little clutch purse with a handkerchief, a rock,

and a crackerjack charm inside. Sometimes, her father
boiled potatoes in the pan they left on the hot plate.

Mostly they boiled weak tea with used teabags
and ate Strongheart dog food from the can.

Because I Never Learned Calculus

I count and multiply everything. I know
numbers, their sound reliability,
their results. I count when I brush,
thirty for each quad, each hundred I walk—
steps to the corner, steps to the mailbox,
steps to the car in the lot. I count grapes
and olives, minutes before rinsing,
seconds before rebooting, 613
pomegranate seeds. I count coins
and cookies, socks and pencils,
hands in the air, faces in the crowd,
words and stitches, hours, months and years.

I cut bread into right angles and quarters,
quilt fabric into rectangles, triangles, trapezoids.
I add fourths and thirds to my batter, double
and divide my recipes, add sums in my checkbook,
calculate unknowns. I count pinches, tads, and dabs,
a bit and some, about so and not quite there. I can make
graphs, enter numbers on spreadsheets.
I can't read the code of formulas, can't figure
slopes or velocity, and I solve for x
in circuitous ways, too many steps,
and no proofs. I will never arrive
at an optimal profit, and a differential
for me is a gear. Change has always been hard
to accept, and I've never understood limits,
but eventually I arrive at what I need.

Chuck

What are we? Humans? Animals? Savages?
   William Golding – *Lord of the Flies*

On the first day of my first class in a tiny room,
Chuck takes a seat so close he taps my desk.
Every day a Polo, dress pants, buttery loafers.

When he looks up, he flashes perfect teeth. He
stares, makes me squirm, but does his work. He's
18. I'm 21. He doesn't treat me as his teacher

ready to discuss *Lord of the Flies*. Behind his silky
voice and Gucci shoes, I see his mean. He instigates
fights and whacks small boys, particularly Juan—

thick horned-rims, buck teeth, chunky—Piggy if he
stepped from the book, and he likes order, logic.
He asks questions, ponders why Jack craves the kill.

The day after spring break, Juan asks for a restroom pass.
A minute later, Chuck dips his face close to mine and asks
to call his mother to bring his lab notes for 4th hour.

You probably wonder how I fell for that. I let him go.
I heard the story after an ambulance took Juan away.
Chuck slammed the bathroom door into Juan's face over

and over until his glasses fell off his broken nose
and cheekbone. Then he plunged Juan's head
into the toilet. By the time the gurney arrived, Juan

was unconscious. Chuck earned his last credits
on Homebound. Juan's parents moved to Texas.
A door had opened into a new darkness. Students

bumped along as that year loomed shadowy
under the care of counselors. A quiet spring
of staring into space. A time of weighing.

Rumors traveled like vapor, like stories of the beast.
We lived in the flicker, the tick. Too many stained
dreams. Too many thoughts about sharpening a stick.

Mark

He never came back after graduation.
When I drive past his former apartment,
I remember his face, hollow from Ramen,
his eyes sunken from nights of formulas
and equations, alone with a chair, a Futon,
and a table he used for a desk. He called
the apartment his Zen island before he
switched on his American Dream, an engineer
far from here. After his classes, he walked
the mile home, and if he needed to go farther,
he biked. My boyfriend Ben was his best friend.
On nights he didn't have class, Ben and I sat
on Mark's floor or at Ben's table, a smoky
haze hanging under his lamp. I wanted
to thank Mark for the night when the cloy
of another's perfume draped over a chair,
and he crossed his arms and glared at Ben.
He whispered words to him I didn't hear. He
looked at me in a way he never had before.
And then he was gone. I heard about the great
new job, but I never saw either of them again.
Mark's still in the doorway, when I drive past,
his jacket slung over a shoulder, the other
leaning against the jamb. The bare bulb
ceiling light still dangles from a black wire.
I remember, like moths remember their lives as
caterpillars, a past better than it ever really was.

Ode to a Male Seahorse

Fins, monkey tail, chameleon eyes,
you're no horse. Your limber
tail can scratch your head,

drape your neck, or hang
on seaweed like a crochet hook
while you vacuum plankton

and tiny shrimp—until your life-long
mate begins the seductive dance.
Together you swirl, blush,

tuck heads, twine tails, flirt,
chirp, hum, snap. Nose to
nose, you form a sea heart.

She drops eggs in your pouch
and wanders off to fatten up.
You tend the nursery. You sleep

in wide-eyed dormancy,
orange in coral,
yellow in sponge.

The day fry swarm in a stream
of apostrophes, hundreds
all at once swirl up

and vanish. Little time
to doze among mangroves
before she returns,

all hums and snaps.

Girls at the Sea Aquarium

Our noses almost touch glass.
Jen, Sue, and I gaze at seahorses
circling inside a wall of water.

The guard says we are lucky, their
twirl and dance almost over. He
calls the male Andy, says we'll see

what few witness, but Jen rushes
to the bathroom to throw up. Nose
to nose the seahorses form a heart.

From green they turn yellow, orange.
Upon her return, Jen says, *It's the size
of a lime*. She sighs and moves closer.

The guard says the seamare deposits
hundreds of eggs, sometimes as many
as 2,000. Jen rushes off again, misses

the head nuzzles, the clutch of tails,
the drop off into the male's pouch.
The pair drift into eel grass. The male

wraps a tail around bits of coral as Jen
returns. The seamare floats off behind
a sponge. Except for daily visits, her part

is done. *No one prepares you for how bad
it's going to get*, Jen says, flushed. Already
the male has covered the eggs with sperm.

For six weeks, he'll regulate blood flow, salt
concentration, oxygen, provide prolactin,
lipids and calcium. *Weeks ago, it was only a bean,*

Jen says. The seahorse will snooze when he can,
hooked to bits of seagrass until the day he expels
hundreds of fry ready to fend for themselves.

At the Allen Ginsberg Poetry Reading

Seeing Allen Ginsberg was the closest I ever came to meeting
Walt Whitman. Allen in the supermarket looking for Walt, me
at ponds channeling Henry David. Allen sat in Kirkwood
auditorium on a roll-in platform, a striped rug under him
and plucked an autoharp next to his lover playing a flute
and wearing only white briefs. Allen wore a tie-dye shirt,
and for a minute we thought we were too early or too late
or someone forgot what to do because the room had no
chairs. Allen sat cross-legged on a rug strumming and humming,
and maybe meditating because his eyes were closed.
The audience looked around, shrugged, sat on the floor,
and wished we had known so we could have brought
a rug like Allen had. After more chanting and music,
Allen recited poems, and his lover played the flute or sometimes
the autoharp, and they stroked their beards, and we were young
and trying to figure it all out but not letting anyone know we
hadn't figured any of it out, and Allen talked to us as though
we were there to have tea and music together and hear poems
even though the room smelled a good deal like weed,
and many eyes looked glassy and red. And the night
went on with Allen talking peace and antiwar and hugging
his lover often. We knew it was a reading like no other we'd
ever see again, and after it ended hours later when someone
came in to say he had to close up, we heard one more poem.
At the door someone was handing out flowers. We left
chatting and thinking bigger thoughts than when we
went in. We stared at the moon and called it mystical,
and now tonight, so many years later, this full moon
on the black water makes me wonder which way
you'd point your beard tonight, Allen Ginsberg.

Cheap Concert Seats

The notes dissolve
like the trail of gardenias
wafting in the neighborhood.
As if viewing binoculars
through the wrong side,
shadow box dancers
move like Punch and Judy
in a box a block away.
Speakers rumble
through us in waves,
voices underwater
or behind a closed door,
as if the Cheshire Cat
were asking, *Did you say
a pig or a fig?*

Thinning the Herd

The child opened the gate.
The child followed the beagle.
The child was lost and hid behind a rock.
The child's ear was infected.
The child no longer wanted oatmeal.
The child drew hearts on the wall.

The child found the gun in the drawer. She'd seen her father shoot pop bottles and cans lined up on the fence. She watched him unload the deer from the top of his car. She watched blood leak from its mouth as her father and his partner carried the deer tied to a pole. When they slit it open, she ran into the house and wept.

The next day she squeezed the kitten too tightly. She cried when it died in her hands. It had been taking all of the milk, the fat one, and she wanted the others to have a chance. *No, no,* she told the white kitten, and its head flopped to the side. It hadn't opened its eyes yet.

She called her mother to fix the white kitten, but her mother said, *You killed it. You killed the healthiest one, the one that looked like its mother.* The mother cat licked and licked the dead one. She carried it to a flowerpot and went back to the living. *See,* the mother said. *She knows it's gone. You have thinned the herd like your father.*

That night the girl dreamed about the kitten. The mother cat morphed into a cat as big as the room and said, *You killed my healthy kitten. You will be punished.* The child screamed, and the father came to the bed. *What's wrong?* he asked.

I killed the white kitten, but it was still the dream, and the father's head became a snake that twisted high into the air and stared at her, its tongue flashing. *You only thinned the herd*, he hissed.

She woke, sweaty. She was five and had committed murder. Her mother no longer allowed her on the porch alone, and the mother cat ran when she saw her.

By the time she was twenty-five, she could still reconstruct the day, the box where the kittens tucked themselves against their mother, the plaid comforter lining the box, the tiny curled paws. She could see the dead one in the flowerpot.

Now, her husband was pushing a pillow into her face Desdemona style. She was going to pay. He knew she had been hiding something, but she did not know what it was. When her husband was burning villages, was he thinning the herd? Ninety percent disabled, he spends days in the back of the barbershop playing poker with old timers and war buddies.

His best friend pulled him off and took the pillow. Air surged again in her lungs, and although she knew it was not her end, it was the end of so many things.

Mother Suite

I. Last Six Months

Methodone has glassed my mother's eyes,
but they watch us pass, watch us dust and set
figurines back in their exact spot. She
is a silent and perpetual brown study
when she isn't watching her tropical fish
or refusing every malt or salad we offer.
It wasn't until after she died that we knew
from the neighbor who sometimes sat with her
that she poured her fresh carrot juice into
the philodendron each day. She no longer
complains of pain, but at night she wakes
my father by knocking on his head to ask him
to get rid of the wall of China circling their bed
or to stop the elves from gambling away our car.
She called the police one night to say our Aunt Lena
was running a drug ring in our living room.
The police insisted they had to search.
My father can no longer carry her as he did
over the threshold when she came home
after surgery. She refuses the wheelchair
but says she can't walk ten steps to the kitchen
from her recliner. My father, wearing his
baseball cap, rolls in his dolly and invites
my mother to climb aboard. She steps
on the platform, leans back, and he taxies
her through the house, dodging the long
oxygen lines. By the time, they reach
the bedroom, I hear her say, *Wheeee.*

II. After the Transfusion

On Saturdays, my father and I attend Italian
classes. I to learn, he to break his dialect.
The three hours we're gone, a neighbor sits
with my mother, now confined to life as far
as oxygen cords can reach. On day two
after her blood transfusion, she perked up
in her chair, a bit of gray fluff sprouting on her
bald head, a punk cancer victim with a paisley
scarf around her neck to cover the hole that never
closed after radiation and surgery. She asked
my father to bring her dresser drawers so she
could touch her things and rearrange them. It'd
been so long. We knew this could take days, but it
was the first time she showed interest in anything
beyond staring at her aquarium fish or wrens hovering
around the feeders. My father lined up six drawers.
She asked for a trashcan and two sacks. As we shuffled
through the door, she was making a pile on each side
of her recliner. *Fresh blood makes me want to do the splits
up the wall*, she said, one of her favorite tricks in the past.
She waved us off. *Stop and have lunch*, she said. *I'm a busy bee
here*. Before we shut the door, she was humming.

III. Chemo

They try to make you comfortable at the clinic,
something to read, television to watch, ear plugs
for your choice of music. They offer a warm blanket
and tuck you in as the bag starts its steady drip.
The first time, my mother cried and said, *This is how
the end begins. I'm only doing this for you and your father.*
After that she shrugged and frowned. She knows
she will throw up for three days and not be able to lift
her head off the pillow. She knows people can't visit.
She asks for the same place each time so she can see birds.
Tomorrow and the next day, I will comb out more hair.
She will never dye her hair again. She will never tell me
how soft her hair still is after all these years. Soon,
it will all rest at the bottom of a brown bag she'll tell me
to toss along with all of the outdated spice tins she's
been sorting through in case she's still here to make
holiday biscotti. *See, I still have my favorite sprinkles.*

IV. Afterward

It's not until I clean out the house after they both
have died that I find it in a cabinet among old photo
albums we rarely opened. For months after my mother
died, my father said over and over, *I know your mother
left something behind. You know how she was.* I did. Always,
she had written little poems or notes and put them
in our lunch boxes, my suitcase, my brother's duffle,
my father's camping gear. My father searched the house,
every drawer, listened to every recording, and probably
looked at the scrapbook and thought it was another
photo album. I found what he never saw. I knew
why she wanted to go through all of her drawers
after the transfusion. She had taken all of the photos
out of an album and turned it into a scrapbook
of everything she'd kept over the years: my brother's
eagle scout award, my father's letter for inventing
a better streetlight, photo of my fencing tournament
victory, every card my dad ever sent her with his
poem inside. I turned page after page, watching
the life she had saved. At the end were letters addressed
to each of us only my brother and I would ever see.

Nulliparous

No swollen ankles,
        no morning sickness,
                no labor pains.

Only the cat's tail
        thumps my stomach
                as he dream twitches.

In friends' houses,
        changing tables replace
                the bookcase or desk.

Antique rockers creak
        with tiny bundles
                cooing in sleep.

I crochet pastel blankets
        and push strollers
                for my nephews,

my friends.
        My cross-stitch sampler
                hangs on a cousin's wall.

I cradle and bounce
        grinning faces of infants
                who go back home.

The yellow baby sweater
        my mother knitted
                fits my niece.

I switch off the light
        knowing only a phone
                or distant train whistle

will wake me. The dog
        pads noiselessly
                through the house.

The Out-of-Town Family Wedding

We've overtaken Motel 6 on Rock Road.
Twenty-five out-of-towners take four days
to complete a wedding. Every room spare
and white, not even a wall print, a whiteness
that keeps its own silence. Each morning,
the Waffle House next door is a flurry
of stacked plates passed over our heads
as we listen to chat between glistening bites
of mapled pancakes. Before we pay, plans
change three times—some leave for shoes
at Macy's, some for the photo shoot, some will
arrange flowers on tables. My husband and I
are thistles underfoot, sticktights tagging along.
We offer to fill cookie trays, assist with fittings,
try to blend as the family shifts and redefines
like an amoeba— my brother and his new wife,
my ex sister-in-law and her new boyfriend.
Without a task, we assign ourselves to snap
photos of everyone, their afternoon shadows
looming behind them. Beer cans stud each day
as groomsmen slosh through fittings, rehearsal,
dinners, and late-night parties in the parking lot.
We shuffle, slam doors, pass around the one
working iron, share the extra scarf that might work,
the brush another forgot. Someone is always going
for more ice, a shower, a nap, a new shirt.
My husband and I lean over the balcony, toast
each other and watch semis grind gears
and wheeze by. Downstairs, Grandma and Grandpa
try to sleep. On Sunday, we load our trunks,
and the convoy heads home, most back in flip-flops,
yawning, anxious for the aspirin to kick in.

Wedding Bouquets

Yesterday's wedding bouquets
                                            are in the dumpster,
their creamy gardenias wilted,
                                            their tea roses
and baby's breath
                                            hang distressed heads,
so quickly the silk and velvet
                                            meet the dark,
the dumpster stinks of yesterday's
                                            salmon
and the thick miasma
                                            of blue cheese
under browned roses as if
                                          an omen of the unsteady

taking the first steps on
                                          wobbly ice skates.

The Drexlers

We talk about extending the fence
where their Jonathan can't drag
his sled across the parsley. We work
on the other side of the house,
away from the hollow dribble
droning until dark. Next door
to the perfect family, we're pariahs
with no children to practice free throws,
dress as Halloween goblins, or slam
volleyballs in games between our houses.
Our phone calls at three a.m. to protest
Biscuit's barking or screeches wafting
from their hot tub gain only a slight *uh-huh*.
In spring, Dad and Alex toss the softball.
Mom plants hybrid iris, and Stacey
practices karate on the patio. By summer,
they all haul rocks for their waterfall
and invite friends to dance between tiki
torches at summer luaus. In fall, Stacey
hikes door-to-door to sell fourteen cases
of World's Finest Chocolate to pay
for cheerleading outfits. In winter, they
carol down the block from a hay wagon,
win first place for their light display.
By August again, they smack croquet balls
into our tomato plants and wrap a striped
muffler around their yard bear before every
football game— until Dad's more frequent
business trips last longer, and the perfect
family sticks up a for sale sign. Mom U-Hauls
off one night into winter darkness with the kids
and leaves Dad with his new coke-snorting paramour.

My Neighbor, Mary Grace, at Six Years Old, Paints Jack-o'-lanterns in Her Driveway

Green and orange tempera, two brushes,
and small cardboard squares surround her.
As I pass with my dog, she says, *The finished ones
are for sale*, and keeps painting. *Four bucks.*
Don't you think that's a little high, I ask? A bead
of orange paint runnels down one she has finished.
She sighs, without looking up, *Well, it's art.*
Oh, yes, I say. *Of course.* She stops to munch
an orange and consider me. Zest sprays the air
and mingles with the eggy odor of tempera
in the hot sun. *In that case, I'll take two*, I say.
She points to the finished ones, some already
cracking in the heat. *Pick the ones you want.*
They are all different. Art has to be that way.
A beetle crawls across the driveway. Green
iridescence flashes. *Ewww*, says Mary Grace
and twists away. *That's art*, I tell her. *Look again.*
No, she frowns. *It's a bug.* She rolls her eyes
and keeps on painting. A crow lands on a branch,
caws, and eyes us. *See*, she says, *even the bird
likes art.* I suggest, *Maybe he wants the beetle.*
She shrugs. I decide the two jack-o'-lantern
paintings will hang in my front window all fall.
I hope she will walk by and see the display. *So,
she says, that will be $4.00 twice. I only take cash.*

Pomegranate

Tart spark of truth.
You harbor rubies.

Hidden nests under rhino
hide scored in quarters.

Open a flared skirt. See
a nursery of celled beads.

Segmented chambers release
teardrops from clustered combs.

Pockets of seeds. They crush.
They bleed. They stain.

They fall like fresh pearls,
baby teeth, scattered dice.

In our mouths they pop,
they stream. They make us

dream. Their antioxidants
heal us. Tart truth. Red truth—

almost sour. A berry with seeds
from the ovary of a single flower.

Cropping

The children learn early. The bravest matadors
kill the bull, cut off its ears, and crowds cheer.

Picadors ride into the Plaza de Toros before fights
to lance the bull's muscles. They gouge and twist

to ensure heavy blood loss, to ensure bulls
can't lift their head. Sometimes, they drug

the bulls, shave their horns to throw them off
balance or rub Vaseline in their eyes. On foot,

banderilleros plunge barbed sticks into the bull
and run him in circles until he stumbles. It is then

the matador arrives in a red-cape flourish to finish
the imminent death. They call this entertainment.

So young to learn of killing for the roar, the purse,
the excitement of the moment, the severed ears

paraded around the ring. Children practice with dogs,
post photos on Facebook, TikTok, holding ears

while their puppies lie bleeding below. Henry VIII
cropped ears for second offenses, Puritans nailed

ears to the pillory for attacking church policy.
Some clay beads are shaped like ears to imitate warrior

necklaces. Owners crop pit bull ears to make them
look tough. Van Gogh never knew his followers

of self-mutilation. Some men and young boys sever
their own ears to look like a skull, to self medicate,

to honor their pain. Do they feel that excitement
of the moment before they quit listening?

Prompt

I ask my students to write a secret
on a slip of paper. *Anything someone*

*might consider a secret. We'll get
ideas for your next story.*

Stacey tilts her head to think.
Brandon looks down at his desk.

Here is a box, I say, *to put them in.*
Can we make some up? *Of course.*

I expect you to make them up.
Can it be someone else's secret?

Yes. Here is my secret.
I fold and toss it in the box.

**Will it still be a secret if we
write a real one?** *Perhaps.*

*Someone might guess
which are true.* **Do we**

have to read our own? *No.*
The box becomes a folded flurry.

You can add more tomorrow.
What if we want to tell a real secret?

Fine. Don't tell me if your secret's true.
I'd be obligated to tell.

Can we read a few today? *Yes.*
My mother is really my sister.

My cousin's in prison, not away at college.
I am not a citizen.

My dad is cheating on my mom.
My mom's boyfriend raped my sister.

That's enough for today.

Brandon Langford Talks through Detention

I'm here because I don't want a suspension,
but I hope you know you caused me to miss my bus.
I don't even understand why I have detention.
You tell us to say what we think. I spoke
my thoughts, and that's my right. My dad
does it all the time, freedom of speech,
and we cheer. Well, we did. He's a combat vet,
but now he's in prison for child porn
and hitting my mom. She's glad he's gone.
Do I have to stay here the whole time?
If I'm nice, can I leave early? You could even
drive me home if you want. My house is four
miles from here. My mom works. You wouldn't
want me to sit outside until ten would you?
I don't know what to write my narrative on.
Maybe you could give me some ideas. Do you
like fish? I have tropical fish. I could write about that.
Have you ever been to a fish show? Bet you
didn't even know there was such a thing.
I won first place in the last show. I set up
a great tank, and all of my fish have babies.
I like guppies best. I once had a mother
die in childbirth, but the baby lived. I still have him.
My fantails are beauties, and I have gouramis
and cichlids. My mom says they calm me down.
You probably want me to shut up and do homework,
write that narrative for your class. I already did my math.
I'm good at math. I'm not good at raising my hand
before I talk. This I know. I can do my timetables
up to fives. My math teacher taught me how to do them
on my knuckles. Do you want me to show you?
Nah, you probably want to grade papers
and ignore me. I get it. My mom does that too.
She turns the tv louder. You wouldn't mind
taking me home would you? You could see my fish.

Disappearing

The first year, Crystal argued about too many exercises,
too many papers, and her attitude outgunned us all.

In a dream I had, someone handed me a baby
wrapped in a soiled blanket. I took it outside to see the stars.

In October, Crystal, pregnant, dropped out of school.
The counselors said nothing. Homecoming distracted us.

When I realized I left the baby outside, I ran back out.
The baby didn't cry. Its lips were blue. It slept deeply.

The next year, Crystal was back in my class. She didn't speak
except when asked a question. She stared into her hands.

She stared into space. Her eyes were buried coins. She came
to my desk to ask what to write about. Tell your story, I said.

I brought the baby back inside to feed it, but its mouth was gone.
A skinny stray roamed the yard. Sniffed where the baby had lain.

To pay off his drug debt, Crystal's boyfriend offered her
for a night as payment. When she fought the dealer,

he shoved a switchblade up her vagina and twisted.
The boyfriend beat her before taking her to the hospital.

I gave the dog a dish of kibble. I rocked the baby in my arms.
Its eyes stayed closed. Parts of it started disappearing.

Tonight on the news, a pregnant woman couldn't drive fast enough
to the hospital. She swerved through a rail and flew into a ditch.

In those airborne moments, she delivered her baby. The police
found the mother's neck broken. The baby rolled under the seat.

Still breathing. One policeman wrapped the cold baby in a soiled blanket and ran to the ambulance through a night frosty with stars.

Crystal didn't bleed to death. Surgery helped. No more sex. No babies. The boys were out on parole. Crystal turned sixteen and told her story.

Ends

> Lord, let us feel pity. . . and sorrow for ourselves
> and all the angel warriors that fall.
> *Fallen Angels* —Walter Dean Myers

What about the end? the teacher asks his seniors.
How has Perry changed in Fallen Angels?

They shrug and look around. One wears
an ankle monitor for robbing Pizza Hut

with his cousin. Several say their fathers
served. Like Perry, they came back different.

Most miss at least one day a week. Most
often suspended or asleep at their desks.

Fourth hour is lunch. On their shift, the boys
talk about fighting, but not war. They talk about

their first time doing time and what to expect—
three meals, cable, heating, and air—far better

than darkness after late shifts at McDonald's.
They talk about sponsors. Each day, the teacher

crosses off a date on his white board calendar.
He twists his ear gauges, these rose gold plugs

bigger than last week's crossbones. He stares
out the window at a broad shadow on the lawn.

What would you have done if trapped? He describes
weekends of body suspension, how it doesn't hurt

as much as they'd think, how his father's
a minister. They nod. He has fifteen piercings.

His arm tats tell a Chinese honor story. On his neck
a red wheelbarrow and white chickens.

Lelia's Hair Museum

Hair bracelets and watch fobs in glass cases form rows of grief.
We gaze at hair earrings, brooches, and lockets clamping snippets of hair.

Hair art hung from a neck, flirted around an arm, before the grievers
died and families passed them on or left them abandoned in old trunks.

Monkeys die from the lack of touch or a mother's love. They will choose
a soft fabric monkey over a metal one full of food. Elephants keen

over ancestral bones, and some birds hover beside a wounded mate.
Mother whales may push their dead baby through waves for weeks before letting go.

When my mother was dying in her hospital bed, I wanted Rolling Thunder to appear
in a chair on the other side of the room to be sure her spirit left safely.

Is grief any less if the mourner is a monkey, a whale, or a dog that shows up
every day at a train station for fourteen years waiting on the soldier to come home?

Last year we celebrated a friend's birthday at the hair museum. This year I found
her grandmother's brooch of braided hair in a broken jewelry box at her estate sale.

Love Should Be More Like Yarrow

One small leaf will speed decomposition
of a wheelbarrow full of raw compost.

Its root secretions activate disease resistance
of nearby plants. It intensifies

medical action of other herbs, a booster
that enhances the power of others. Meant

to heal, it staunches cuts and wounds, aids
colds, and fevers. Blood cleanser. Easer

of toothaches. Drought tolerant. Content
to live in pastures, embankments, roadsides,

waste ground, and from a ditch, it waves
to us with its feathery foliage and yellow blooms.

Saturdays at the Bakery

The couple picked a bagel
and an oatmeal cookie larger
than a splayed hand. Coffee.
One endless cup, steaming
its notes around them
like a harbor fog while they
stared through the window
to watch the spill
of the gumball's spiky seeds
or the flutter of white
and pink tree blossoms.
They weren't headed
to a black tie fundraiser
at the Hilton, weren't
planning an Alaska cruise
or a trip to Majorca.
The cookie, the bagel,
the coffee, the window
were enough.

Women Talk of Men They've Known

Women in this room are listening
to one of us tell about the man

who asked to stroke her knees
but wanted nothing more.

Another remembers sexy phone chats
with a boy who never asked her to dance,

never took her to Big Boy for chocolate malts.
He told her she did not live up to his future.

One remembered the stiff shove of the screen
lifting, the long legs of a man scraping,

waggling over the ledge, until the police
coaxed him back into a squad car.

The next week he straddled his Harley below
her window even though police told him

to move on. He said it wasn't illegal
to sit, to watch stars, to take in night air.

A stranger opened my car door the night
I waited in the church lot for a friend.

She was late from being with the man
she didn't marry, and we had to go home together.

Moonlight caught the blade the stranger flashed
as I slipped out the other door and ran across a field.

In the room where we tell these secrets, I
wonder if the silent ones are holding back,

their fingers circling a thumbnail of memory,
too deep, too immovable for speech.

Cataract Surgery

> *The history of eyes, like their anomalies,*
> *is written on the retina, in every image stored*
> *and every stunning line of record.* —Madeline Defrees

Lined up on gurneys, we wait in half-light
for the needle's drip to drift us like kites,

away from dwelling on the slip of a scalpel,
the tightness of a ligament to hold. We wait

for clouds to lift, halos and stars to fade like final
notes, a curtain to open on a clear stage.

Over in seven minutes, we awake, wobbly,
and step from the amber varnish of a dark

Rembrandt, into the new blue of a Hockney morning
where seeing is believing in all of its bright white.

Fracture

Like sun on dark water,
I am sudden,

quiet as oysters and time's unspoken breath.
Hot water on ice. Hammer tap on a mirror.

I skate into action, scrim windowpanes,
spiderweb windshields, triple strike

a shoulder. I'm the moment
after the car wreck,

the snag of a foot on a stair,
the pitch into the dark.

Unwritten Rules

Don't think about going down that street, Sandy said.

That street? I pointed. *My brother went to the high school on this corner years ago,* and she said, *Yeah, but that was then. Just let me off at the corner.*

What's going to happen if I drive you home? I asked.

Your car won't come back out like it went in.
See that glass in the street. See that trash can fire?
Nothing friendly about protesting here.

What about you? I asked.

They won't hurt me, she said.

I let Sandy out at the corner by Central High
and headed back down 40 Hwy towards home
where once no black students went to my school,

where I was the lone outcast in a sea of wasps
who'd already picked their friends, together
since kindergarten. Who called me wop.

Now, years later, Central's new high school has
an indoor pool, far nicer than the pool my brother
competed in to earn a scholarship. Lou's Drug replaced

with a Quick Trip. Vacant lot where my house stood.
A highway project divided the neighborhood and tore
down my grade school and blocks of houses.

When I told my mother I wanted Sandy as a bridesmaid
in my Italian wedding with dancing and all the aunts baking
biscotti for the dinner, she said it wouldn't look right.

Italian girls, she said. *Your own kind.* That meant cousins.
That meant a high-necked bridal dress and a long mantilla
because no respectable Italian girl would do otherwise. Years later,

riots started up again on the same street. I visited Sandy
at her new house, and she said I couldn't come back. Her
partner didn't want her hanging out with a white woman.

Barbed

Someone has left open
a mailbox fronted
with barbed wire
twisted into a nest.
Six vellum notes lay
stacked and stamped.
A spider's web,
woven across the wire
like a torn door screen,
has captured a fly, a moth,
and a hornet still thrashing.
Who will reach in there?

I didn't cry when I watched
my father sew together
where barbed wire
tore open my cat's throat.

Atop the mailbox,
a starling eyes me
and tilts its head.
The air steals breath.
Gum trees toss spiky balls.
Last year, they caused
my dog and me to fall twice.
Worry, no more certain
than a torn sack hanging
from a bush, cannot save us.

Losing Cousin Carolyn

The news came via Facebook. Simple obit.
Immediate family only. This is the age of Covid.
This is the time of dying alone. Grieving alone.

We sat in a funeral home pew the last time I saw
Carolyn, cousins lined up together as we always are
when we say goodbye, in that case to our last uncle.

Despite opposite views, we shared a life together,
weddings, reunions, death. A time to share family
stories or photos we found in a parent's basement.

I imagine her sons, graveside with their father,
no chairs, no flower sprays, no family circling them.
Her brother hundreds of miles away, kidneys failing.

I drive past the house where they lived when we
played Fish or paper dolls on her bedroom floor.
It seems so small. The shutters and window box sag.

A vacant birdhouse sways near an empty feeder. A clump
of limp jonquils wave, and their old Dragon's Blood Sedum
I loved pokes through the broken arms of a gargoyle.

Dreaming through Covid

Most nights I dream of the dead,
my mother telling me, my father agreeing,

that we all feel afraid sometimes.
That's what the counselors tell us.

I rescued a dog but she bit my friend.
Someone is dreaming about her daughter.

I want my mother to come back
to dream about me. I stand in a crowd,

and everyone offers me caviar, wine,
and crisp crusts with smoked salmon.

Will someone find me when I die?
My nephew called to say he dreamed

about his Nonny and Papa, about going
to their house on Sunday, but I wasn't there.

He said that he didn't want me to die
until I gave him Nonny's red sauce recipe.

Today the peace plant unfurled two new
cupped white heads, shiny and perfect.

Only two days ago, I considered, its leaves
tiresome, moving it downstairs.

House Dreaming

Twice I drove by my old house during Covid
to see if it had adapted to its latest owners.

Was this now their nest for future dreaming,
for finding places to hide and remember spaces?

Sometimes I dream about our other house without
an attic but with a labyrinth for a basement,

rooms for playing dress up, the loud furnace
room. The workshop and closet of bottles,

the house urban renewal tore down. A house
wraps itself around you. You can still go there,

and its walls hold you up even when the rooms
are gone. The place you live keeps the rain out,

keeps the sun off your skin, but offers its windows
to watch the sun set where your cousin

is gathering up dolls whose hair she bobbed.
After you leave a house, you can still see

where your mother buttered toast or where you kept
the bread on the refrigerator so the cat wouldn't

eat holes in the bag. In the pantry, you can see
the applesauce on the shelf with the extra bottle

of ketchup, the knives lined up perpendicular
in their drawer. You can see the morning glories,

the way cooks look out windows as they stir batter
to be sure the dog hasn't jumped the fence. You can

see the yellow sponge in the bathtub, your brush
on the sink. You can see the way light slants through

the basement window near the furnace's glow when it kicks on,
in harmony with all irrationality of depths and empty space.

Socially Distancing, We Buy Plants Too Early

The basil, rosemary, and dill, snug
in their nursery flats, wanted more space,
and cosmos, those coddled preemies,
already sent up stalks in search of more sky.
At least that's what I told myself as I tucked
them into my cart, but I knew it was too
soon for them to leave their hot house
clime for frosty nights, frisked by wind.
In two weeks, hundreds of arms would reach
for the same parsley plant, same lantana, line up
six feet apart with their carts of tomatoes, dill,
knock-out roses, and variegated hosta. Each night
we brought in the basil, the lacy coleus, the fragile
ferns, and let them watch the others huddled
in pots, wearing white plant covers, their temporary
tombs. Cold little ghosts swaying in moonlight.

Auld Lange Syne's End of Set

That last shot of tequila induces
head spins in the parking lot, makes us
wish for Tuesday or take backs.

We wake to the unfamiliar, learn the art
of exit, face the red-eye, drive past car
wrecks, cross icy bridges of thought.

Last words spurt forth, microbursts
ugly as cold sores, cause for signing
papers, clearing out drawers.

In twenty years, they'll roll their eyes
when we knit, wonder if winter's
darkness exhaled us whole.

We wave sparklers on the home lawn,
let the New Year slide in early with
stories we trade like sports cards,

stories we can choose,
more butter each year,
smooth and full in the mouth.

We lift the wine to toast—
that hint of black cherry,
that crisp structured finish.

Fortune Tellers

The thin, red, translucent fish
bends and wiggles in my hand.

It is not a miracle, is not a fish,
is flat as paper. It curls as it grabs

and changes molecules to let me
know its fortune-telling truth.

The mood ring on my finger
shifts from green to yellow to blue

as though its liquid crystals know
more than I do about how I feel.

The Mexican jumping bean moth
hidden in its tiny piñata

springs across my palm.
Someone says I make him dance

because I make him hot.
The die floating in a blue solution

of the Magic 8 Ball
tells me over and over

Don't count on it,
Don't count on it.

Wine Club

I'm learning wine ethos, terms: terroir
and tannins, vinification and lees. Most days,
new choices like a friend saying, *Try this
jammy Zin, or this pinafore-crisp Savignon
Blanc.* I wait for a velvet mouth, tongue zip.
Old words carry new meaning: structured,
up front, opulent, bung and blush, a long way

from jugs of plonk. I'm gleaning a perfect sniff,
an impeccably refined mouth roof, never quite
expecting spice cake, eucalyptus, layers of forest
floor and aromas of bracken to be a desire or to drink
only generous wines with big enough personality
to entertain the neighbors next door and allow
for fig paste, cigar box, and a long mulled finish.

The pale salmon Rosé's floral expression has lead tonic
notes of lilac, underpinned by violets and rosemary
with full support of strawberry, melon, and lavender
like small but memorable parts in a play, true definition
in palate language and stroked with a spine of minerals—
served best on cool nights around modest breezes,
a firepit, and a nod to mussels or littleneck clams.

On Tuesday, I can order a golden Chardonnay
with a long finish, possibly into tomorrow, of baked
apple, vanilla, hazelnut cream, and pie spices. Fruit
heavy with layers of melon, pineapple marmalade,
pear, and lemon chiffon in a butter cream texture,
so decadent it should accompany fresh crab and lobster,
a skimpy swimsuit, and a Cayman Island exotic scuba dive.

Wednesday offers a good nose sniff into a plucky
Pinot Noir, its perfectly balanced spices born
with the wind and accented with violet notes,
wild thyme, lavender, plum, and cherry. Despite its
tight entry, it unfurls to its promised fleshy, satin
finish. It will leave you with one arm hanging
off the couch and another full glass in the other.

Delivery boys smile when they boost the bottles
across my threshold, perhaps happy to meet
someone with a good nose, a trained mouth roof
grateful to embrace a perky cinnamon and cedar Cab
with lush black cherry and mulberry bursts nuanced
with an underbrush of sweet tobacco and brambly notes
yet perfectly structured to hold up a sirloin or braised ribs.

A very attractive 97 pt. juicy showstopper with vibrant
aroma and balanced hints of fresh herbs, pepper, baking spice,
wild balsam, and aromatic sandalwood is an envied discovery.
Old-vine Grenache from climes of Aragon dominates the blend
with extra backbone from Cab and Syrah's acidic lift. With its
core of cherries and berries and spiced biscuit aroma, this blend
is sleek, arresting, and smoothly delivered on any tongue.

For afternoon lunches with friends, Vouvray delights
with its fruity charm of poached quince, sliced golden
apples, and Bosc pear enhanced by jasmine, plum, wet
river rocks, and nectarines. The mineral tones lean in
through the finish. Electric minerality curls nicely around
a grilled shrimp salad with sorbet and leaves the palate
refreshed. Its nose bouquet will demand a second glass.

So through winter, I'm training with so many to learn:
Malbec, Merlot, Riesling, Prosecco, Zinfandel, Syrah. It takes
months to appreciate meatiness and sparkle, to recognize notes
of tapenade, crushed flower buds, licorice and cassis, to know
perfect tightrope balance, but I am a dedicated student committed
to the task. I sip and sniff through falling snow and icy roads.
By spring, who knows? Perhaps a sotted pro.

Lost in the Snow

We have circled the area for hours, unsure
where we are on the map, and when we are sure,
not sure how to get where we're going to view
cathedrals and broken marbles in alcoves, and it's
snowing, flakes laying a little carpet around us as we
search for a way out, a way back into a clearing while
one of us keeps looking at a map as we single-file
down narrow streets leaving a snow trail and see
a train station where we can board as soon as we
figure out where it will take us while the snow
falls and keeps falling and icing the tracks, engines
struggling and wheezing, a distant whistle, wind
swirling snow, and snow covering benches, and sky
is paper, a few birds scratching marks, one leaving
hieroglyphs on the ground beside us as we look
at the map and see nothing we know but know
that some time before long we'll be somewhere
we want to go as the snow keeps falling and falling.

II

Considering the Alternatives   Maryfrances Wagner

Jackson Pollock's One

The spider has woven
me in or out. Its
messy tangle,
a crisscross
of broken limbs,
ice storm debris,
an angry canopy
of pen scribble,
a black and white
net, the pale fade
of blue and green,
epicenter of red.
I transcend crisscross,
tangled string, black
whorl on white.
Black on me.

Jackson Pollock's One   Maryfrances Wagner

Island

I, a rootless, floating island,
redolent of basil, sage, and thyme.
I watch night, randomly studded,
settle like a hen, a rhyme.

I fall into the basement
of never-used dreams
listen to the hiss of the sea
and none of this is about me.

Island   Maryfrances Wagner

August

Another notch
on a post—the way

too much water kills grass
in its slow, steady runnel

its stagnant snag. You're
the swollen door that no longer

clicks, like a relationship that lost
its way before anyone knew, now

as impenetrable as a lowered
blind. Only the dog comes in

smelling of sunlight, his black
fur aglitter, his pupils wide.

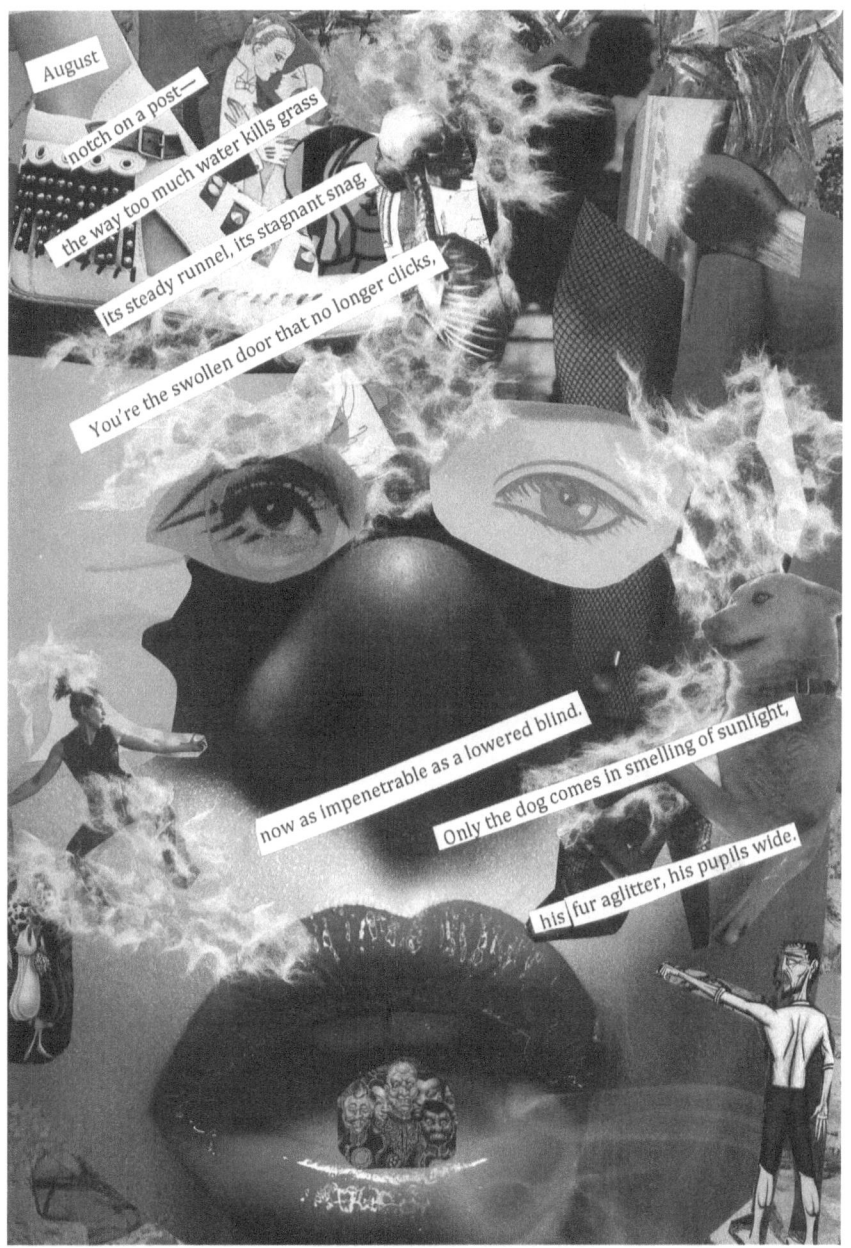

August   Maryfrances Wagner

III

This small wilderness

Rare   Maryfrances Wagner

Missouri

Little Blue Trace, still as glass all winter,
breaks its silence to eel around its curves.

Sunlight spangles the surface like a flash
of minnows. Mayapples open their umbrellas

and shade trillium. The hunt is on for morels
hidden under elms. A bluebird skims below a heron

flapping to its rookery. The chorus frogs creee
and trill. I stretch my arms to the cave state,

start of the Pony Express, rolling hills
and river bluffs, prairie and plateau, earth

solid beneath my feet. Summer brings
the thump of June bugs on lights, honeybees,

and the hornworm emerges as a sphinx moth.
By July we wipe sweat from our necks and bite

into sweet corn and catfish, the plumpest Big Boys,
and juicy Red Havens. Pawpaws and persimmons

slip from their trees in thuds until katydids
cease their churning, and chill scatters us

like the red and yellow leaves backlit
in the last October light. Frost returns to scrim

our windows and silence the Little Blue Trace
again. We watch snow erase former

impressions. By morning, the reverse braille
of bird tracks will leave us runic messages.

Look deep into nature, and then you will understand everything better. ~Albert Einstein

Man's heart away from nature becomes hard. ~Standing Bear

Stay Close   Maryfrances Wagner

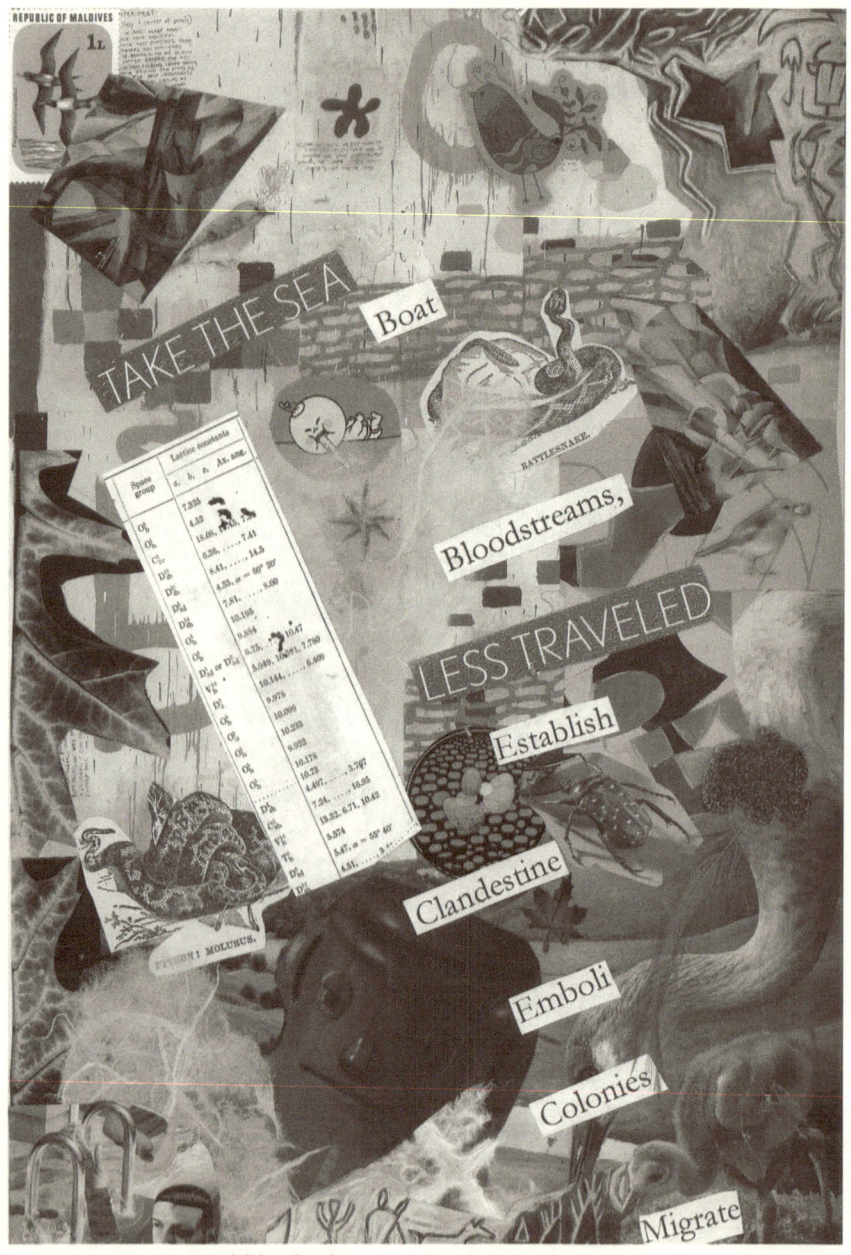

Take the Sea Maryfrances Wagner

Garage Pantry Moths

The cake mix squirms.
A flutter of wings
stumble through stringy
webs and flour.
The muffin mix
is the same—and
the cornmeal. Webs
drape the pasta
still in its clear
wrap—everything
lost in the pantry.
We didn't see
them flutter in
or lie flat, still
as stuck leaves
against walls. Where
were we while they
shrank into slivers
and shivered through
the closed door
into darkness.

Rain Haibun

While the weathervane spins, unable to offer a direction, the rain increases and does not stop. It rushes downward, drags limbs, plastic bags trapped in twigs, a blue cup, a bloated squirrel. It rushes onto the walking trail, parks a canoe, and yanks up sand and silt as it surges on. It uproots weak trees and berried bushes. The creek banks and flushes gravel down the trail's long tongue. The water we prayed for has descended, fills the parched cracks zigzagging across open field and across yards and gardens, and nothing stops it.

> The garden tomato
> ready to pick splits
> and oozes its sweet seeds.

The Pogo Cat Haibun

Someone hit the cat and drove on. It bounced in the street like a pogo stick, straight up, over and over, each time hitting its head on the asphalt. Its paralyzed back leg did not move, its head oozed, and each time it hit, it wailed. Unable to move forward to where the grass may have accepted it more like a trampoline, it banged and bounced into whatever spot the force of its body pushed—in the path of cars, down the ramp toward the freeway. Up and down, up and down, its meows a long shout into where it was going, but it did not stop, and it did not stop, and then

>   the sun reached
>   the horizon and swallowed
>   the last meow.

Will

Today the dog refused to move
from a clump of dead leaves.
It was choke her or let her sniff
whatever vole might sleep below.

Will is a stone too heavy, a long-distance
drive. When we adopted her, she ran
away for eight days. On night patrols
we saw her thunder up the middle

of the road, spotlighted by streetlights.
One night three of us cornered her
in a strip mall before she bolted
into the darkness of sticktights.

We kept the gate open. The water
and salmon we left were gone each morning,
but the trap we set only fooled a raccoon.
Neighbors spotted her behind the dumpsters,

lying in awning shade, or crossing the highway.
On the ninth morning, she rose from a pile
of leaves in the yard, barked, and came
in the house as though nothing had happened,

sitting sphinx-like, paws tucked
under her, her eyes unreadable.

For What We Don't Know

I am unsure of the world, but my dog reads
what's underground, what lingers around trees.
She lives by what she hears lurking in spaces we don't know.

Tonight the sunset will expose thin, broken limbs
and gild them in a certain glow
before day dissolves and winks again.

For all trees losing ground,
for all passersby, our porch light—
mystery of blue haze and a small arch—gleams

for the dog tilting her ear, for birds, for the moon
hiding its stars and silvering the snow.

Naked

The amaryllis drops
its red dresses.
I find them crumpled
in the morning,
left from whatever
happened while we slept.
No putting them back on now.

The Christmas cactus
is no better
at keeping her clothes on,
little handkerchief skirts
scattered and limp.
In this drafty house,
how can they stay
so comfortably naked?

Fabulous Realities

Two things that do not belong together touch in some way.
— Ken McCrorie

1. Rush Hour Protection

A child gripping a red
suitcase and a bald
man sniffing a rose
from a wheelchair
take their chances crossing
a five-lane highway. An
American flag flaps
from a long skinny stick
taped to the wheelchair. When
the man turns his face toward us,
only stopping distance
between us, his silver
tooth glints in the late sun
before they roll across.

2. The Nest

An upheaved nest
landed upside down.
A slick smear runs
from a broken blue egg.
Woven through nest twigs,
a York Patty wrapper,
a wad of brushed dog hair,
and clumps of dryer lint.

3. Pit Bull

The pit bull plops meaty
flanks in the mulch and stares
into the west like a gunslinger
with crinkled brow. His
flapped ear twitches
as the wind stirs. He turns
and shields an injured rabbit
with a soft paw.

Ghost Forest

> Found in *The New Yorker*

Among the missing
are the lobsters.

We don't know
what we don't know.

Trees swallowed by fire—
dead as telephone poles.

Disappearing before our eyes—
bear, wolf, cougar—

reminder of what was here
and now is not.

Maple and sweet-gum,
creek, snapping turtles,

hawks, bald eagles,
red-backed salamanders,

cod bigger than a man.
We accept what we know.

Cockeyed, crooked,
scars and burrs,

seriously dead, grayer
and grayer.

Victims, dissenters,
birds.

After Adopting Sylvie

A north wind outsings summer, shocks
leaves into freefall, blackens herbs,
reminds our rescued dog that once
she made her way on ditch water,
careless mice, and spilled trash;
dug leaf beds deep enough that wind
and rain and people didn't find her.

Only her collapse made it possible
to loop a leash, shoot her with antibiotics,
label her unadoptable, and pass her
from shelter to shelter, far away
from the family that left her
on a country road, where they hoped
someone would take her home.

Today, after a woods walk, Sylvie zooms
the yard, a breath away from snagging
the chipmunk that stumbled out from
under a brick and flashed across the yard.
She's a hackle and haste hunter, but the chipmunk
dives into a hole. We call her, but she stares
into the wind, feral Sylvie back on the road.

Rabbits

Rabbits in the wild often die
within a year. The kits in our yard

lived three weeks. My heeler, Emily,
guarded the nest, protected them

from hawks, a calico, a fox
and even her brother, Pablo.

I only wanted them to go away.
Too many years of basil, parsley

and lettuce gnawed to nubs. I
swallowed darkness like a smooth

merlot, and carried the kits into the woods.
Their small feet thumped in my palm.

I took a breath and struck them with a rock
until squirm and squeal were gone.

I learned yesterday that within hours
of giving birth, rabbits can get pregnant

again and that the smell of predators
or loud shrieks can cause them

to die of shock. If I had only known
I could have screamed the kits to death.

The Deer

The deer work their way down the easement
behind our houses, chomping twigs and new leaves.
We watch eight mill and crunch acorns. They come
daily, sometimes in pairs or quartets, but rarely alone.

One morning, six sprinted across our yard. The mottled doe
huffed and swished a flash of white. A front leg was broken.
As she shuddered, the broken part twirled. She stitched
her way through the wooded easement. The others
followed. I watched until they were gone.

Last year, a three-legged deer limped through summer, always
last in her little herd. I watched her munch chicory
with the others. Saw her triple prints on the trail
until the day she wasn't fast enough and lay open-eyed
in the street. The next morning only a blood map left behind.

They say a deer can heal from a broken leg, sometimes so well
she won't limp. One night a doe's barking woke me, and I
couldn't help but think it might be the doe with the broken
leg. All summer, I watched for her. I wanted her to have healed
so well I wouldn't recognize her among the others.

Mushroom Squad

Overnight, eight
white mushrooms
have emerged—
a squad umbrellaed for rain.
We examine them in our yard,
our pack of four,
two rescued dogs carrying
their damage like loaded
backpacks. The dogs want
to sniff for information.

Leave them alone, my husband
says. *In this heat, they will
be gone by noon.*

Tonight from the window,
they are glowing in the dark,
covered in moonlight,
opening their umbrellas wider,
and tomorrow they will still
be there and the next day
waiting for their orders.

Those Left Behind

During mating season, the barred owls,
woke us every night. An abandoned
nest now. Someone barreled over them
while they fed on a dead squirrel.

Last spring, a mother skunk left her den
to walk her kits for the first time, a waddle
of three behind her. Striped tails in the air,
they imitated her swish and sway.

The next day, the mother lay splayed
on the path like a biology dissection.
An afternoon wind spilled redbud blossoms
over the owls before they disappeared.

Someone on the neighborhood blog says a mother
fox is nursing babies under her deck, worries they
will kill her dog. A dozen of us say her dog is safe.
Forty suggest ways to get rid of the foxes.

Last week, a car hit a buck crossing the highway.
The buck dragged itself to an empty knoll and stared
ahead. The next day, the buck was gone, but a cyclist
was directing his dog down the same highway, past

the same knoll, depending on hand signals
to keep the dog following its master, the afternoon
sun in their eyes, the traffic heavier than usual
when the cyclist took a left turn.

Myotis Lucifugus

> Brown cave bats [are] critical pollinators. . . .
> They eat thousands of insects in a single night,
> and their pest-control value to the economy is
> estimated in the tens of billions of dollars.
> —*Defenders of the Wilderness*

During the Wednesday blizzard,
you posted a photo of an ice-covered
bat hanging from your screen door.

You didn't rescue it, glad
to see it fly off into sleet,
as though it might recover,

as though bats might be infinite.
On summer nights, tunnels of wings
pour into the sky. A ledge shadow opens,

a stir near a face, a dark leaf passing.
Brains small as beans, bats hear
beetles crawl, moths fly.

With a wing, they shawl themselves
or cradle their one pup they can locate
among the squawking thousands.

In their hibernaculum, they
toe hang, closed umbrellas, quiet
as glistening nuns, unless a gunshot

deafens or a light beam frightens them
to drop their pup to the cave floor where
hungry coachwhips scuttle over bones.

Natural Songs   Maryfrances Wagner

Raccoon on the Path

> ... nearly two thirds of the sensory data that
> [a raccoon is] processing comes from
> cells that interpret various types of touch
> sensation. In other words, touch is as
> important a sense as hearing, smell, and
> sight.
> —*Northern Woodlands*

A toad, small as a pencil eraser, bounces
across the path like a lost bead. The turtle,
halted by our footsteps, closes all doors.
We count eleven bird songs, find buckeye,
bluebird feather, spotted eggshell.

One morning, a raccoon—destroyer
of our dog's dish, eater of our neighbor's
goldfish, thief of tomatoes, break-in artist
of garbage—is in the throes of his end.

He lies in the narrow part of the path, already
his cloudy eyes drifting into what's next. He
doesn't drag himself away. He curls
his fingers in and out, his sensors.

On the second day, he pulls a sycamore leaf
over his face, as though he's covered himself
so we can't see his private death. My husband
says, *Don't touch him.* We step around him. We step

around him on the third day, and again he pulls
the leaf over his face and raises his hand, palm
toward us like a traffic cop, then curls his fingers
in and out. The frogs chirr. What gift

is compressed in this small wilderness, these
last moments. We can't improve the situation.
We spread leaves over him.

The fourth morning a dark, wet
impression haunts the path.

The Key

solving for x…3/x+x/b =4b

solving for x…3/옷+유/b =4b

solving for x…3/x+ 🐢 /b =4b

solving for x…3/x+🐦/b =4b

solving for x…3/x+🐘/b =4b

solving for x…3/x+🐟/b =4b

solving for x…3/x+🦊/b =4b

solving for x…3/x+🐒/b =4b

solving for x…3/x+🐞/b =4b

solving for x…3/옷+x/b =4b

solving for x…3/x+🐫/b =4b

solving for x…3/🌳 +x/b =4b

Here   Maryfrances Wagner

Maryfrances Wagner's books include *Salvatore's Daughter, Light Subtracts Itself, Dioramas, Pouf, The Silence of Red Glass, The Immigrants' New Camera*, and *Red Silk*, winner of the Thorpe Menn Book Award. Poems have appeared in *New Letters, Laurel Review, Rattle, Voices in Italian Americana, Main Street Rag, River Styx, Vox Populi, Journal of American Poetry, Birmingham Poetry Review, Louisville Review, Poetry East, Unsettling America: An Anthology of Contemporary Multicultural Poetry* (Penguin Books), *Literature Across Cultures* (Pearson/Longman), and *The Dream Book, An Anthology of Writings by Italian American Women* (winner of the American Book Award from the Before Columbus Foundation) as well as many others. She co-edits the *I-70 Review*, co-edited the *Whirlybird Anthology of Greater Kansas City Writers* and *Missouri Poets: An Anthology*, has served as President of The Writers Place and secretary on the KC Creates Board of Directors. She was the 2020 Missouri Individual Artist of the Year and serves as Missouri's 6th Poet Laureate (2021-2023).